SWEET VALENTINES
EASY-TO-MAKE TREATS, CARDS & CRAFTS

table of contents

© Disney Enterprises, Inc. *Disney FamilyFun* is a trademark of Disney Enterprises, Inc.
For more great ideas, subscribe to *FamilyFun* magazine at www.familyfun.com/magazine.
Published by Dalmatian Press, LLC, in conjunction with Disney FamilyFun Group. **Printed in China.**
The Dalmatian Press name is a trademark of Dalmatian Press, Franklin, Tennessee 37067. 1-866-418-2572.
No part of this book may be reproduced or copied in any form without the written permission from the
copyright owner. All rights reserved. CE14034 Disney FamilyFun Valentine Treats and Crafts

sweet heart pops

MAKES: 6 | **PREP TIME:** 20 MINUTES | **BAKING TIME:** 10 MINUTES

Spread some love on Valentine's Day by handing out these white-chocolate-filled candy canes.

YOU WILL NEED

- 12 mini candy canes
- 6 (6-inch) paper lollipop sticks
- ½ cup white chocolate chips
- 1½ teaspoons vegetable oil
- Red, white, and pink nonpareils or sugar sprinkles

1. Heat the oven to 235°. On a parchment-lined baking sheet, arrange the candy canes as hearts and bake them for 10 minutes.

2. Slide the hearts, still on the parchment paper, onto a work surface. Quickly pinch each heart onto a lollipop stick as shown below (an adult's job).

3. In the microwave, melt together the chocolate chips and the oil in 10-second intervals, stirring between heatings.

4. Spoon the chocolate mixture into the center of each heart, then top with non-pareils or sugar sprinkles. Cool the pops before serving or wrapping them. We packaged our sweet heart pops in lollipop bags purchased at a craft store.

sweet treats

MAKES: 8-12 | PREP TIME: 30 MINUTES | BAKE TIME: 20-25 MINUTES

What do you get when you mix graham cracker crumbs and chocolate chips? Love at first bite. You're sure to earn brownie points with your valentines if you whip up a batch of these heart-shaped treats.

YOU WILL NEED

- ❏ 36 (2-inch) graham crackers
- ❏ 1 (14-ounce) can sweetened condensed milk (don't use evaporated milk)
- ❏ 2 teaspoons vanilla extract
- ❏ ¼ teaspoon salt
- ❏ 1 (6-ounce) package semisweet chocolate chips
- ❏ ¾ cup coarsely chopped pecans

1. Preheat the oven to 350° for metalware or 325° for glassware. While you generously grease an 8-inch square baking pan, put your kids to work crushing the graham crackers into fine crumbs. It's especially easy and fun if you seal the crackers in a plastic bag and then use a rolling pin.

2. Next, stir together the sweetened condensed milk, vanilla extract, and salt in a large mixing bowl. Add the chocolate chips, pecans, and graham cracker crumbs, and mix with a wooden spoon until well blended.

3. Spoon the batter (it will be very stiff) into the greased pan. Use the back of a wooden spoon (or clean hands) to pat the batter into an even layer. Bake for 20 to 25 minutes. Let cool completely in the pan.

4. Finally, use a cookie cutter or a butter knife to cut out small—these brownies are rich!—heart shapes. Serve plain or with a scoop of vanilla ice cream or raspberry sherbert.

heartfelt pancakes

Send your loved ones off to school and work with an especially sweet morning spread.

1. Check party or discount stores for red, pink, or purple table covers, place mats, plates, plasticware, or napkins.

2. For a centerpiece, look for red or pink flowers at your local florist or grocery store.

3. Surprise your family with personal valentines or love notes at each place setting.

4. Serve heart-shaped pancakes. Use a measuring cup with a spout or a plastic bag with one corner cut off to pour or pipe pancake batter onto the griddle in a heart shape. Serve with whipped cream and colorful fruits such as raspberries, strawberries, or cherries.

heartwarming pizza

What's the fastest way to your family members' hearts? Through their stomachs! Serve Valentine's Day meals with expressions of affection. Breakfasts can feature pancakes shaped like X's and O's, and lunches can feature heart-shaped sandwiches and pink milk shakes. And at dinnertime, shape pizza dough into a heart and finish it with your family's favorite toppings.

jello treats

This lovely dessert is easily assembled by chilling layers of gelatin and condensed milk. Even sweeter, it's low-fat.

YOU WILL NEED

- ☐ 3 (3-ounce) packages of red, flavored gelatin
- ☐ 2 (¼-ounce) envelopes of unflavored gelatin
- ☐ 1 (14-ounce) can of sweetened condensed milk

1. Dissolve one package of red gelatin in ¾ cup boiling water. Add ¾ cup cold water, then pour the mixture into a 9- by 13-inch glass pan and refrigerate for 1 hour.

2. Stir together ½ cup boiling water and the condensed milk. In a separate bowl, dissolve all the unflavored gelatin in ½ cup cold water for 1 to 2 minutes. Thoroughly mix in ¾ cup boiling water, then combine this mixture with the milk and let it cool. Add half the mixture to the pan of red gelatin, pouring it over a spatula to slow the stream, and refrigerate for 20 minutes.

3. Continue alternating layers—gelatin mix, the remaining milk mix, the final gelatin mix— chilling each for 20 to 30 minutes to set it. Create individual servings with a heart-shaped biscuit or cookie cutter.

rose cupcakes

MAKES: 12 CUPCAKES | **PREP TIME:** 30 MINUTES

You don't need to have a green thumb—or be a florist—to share these beautiful blooms. They're made from spirals of Fruit by the Foot fruit leather centered on mini cupcakes. Here's how to arrange your own bouquet.

YOU WILL NEED

❑ 12 mini cupcakes
❑ White icing
❑ Clean scissors

❑ 6 rolls of Fruit by the Foot fruit leather in Cherry Rage or Strawberry flavor
❑ 1 roll of Fruit by the Foot fruit leather in Green Apple Wave flavor

1. Frost 12 mini cupcakes with white icing.

2. To make a rose, unroll a piece of the cherry or strawberry fruit leather and divide it in half along the wavy perforated middle line. Take one of the halves and roll up about 5 inches to form the flower's center. Set the rolled strip wavy side up in the middle of a cupcake, as shown, and continue to loosely wrap the remaining fruit leather around the center at a slight angle until the flower is completed.

3. Repeat this process for the remaining flowers. (You should be able to get 2 mini roses out of each roll of fruit leather.)

4. Cut leaf shapes from the wavy edge of the Green Apple Wave strip as shown, then tuck the leaves under the roses.

white hot chocolate

A dash of pudding mix turns a winter favorite into an extra-special treat.

YOU WILL NEED

❑ 1½ tablespoons white chocolate-flavor instant pudding mix

❑ 1 cup milk

❑ Whipped cream

❑ Crushed peppermint candies or candy canes (for garnish)

1. For each serving, combine the pudding mix and the milk in a microwavable mug, then heat the mixture in the microwave for 60 seconds on high.

2. Top with a dollop of the whipped cream and bits of the crushed peppermint candy.

pink banana smoothie

SERVES: 2 | **PREP TIME:** 10 MINUTES

Who says kids won't eat tofu? They'll slurp it up and ask for more after one taste of this sweet, good-for-you smoothie.

YOU WILL NEED

❑ 1 cup apple juice or cider

❑ 2 ounces soft silken tofu (about ¼ cup)

❑ 1 cup frozen strawberries

❑ 1 frozen very ripe medium banana

1. Blend all the ingredients together until smooth.

2. Pour into fancy glasses.

3. Slip in a straw. Serve for Valentine's Day.

SMOOTHIE TIPS

· For added nutrition, slip in low-fat protein, such as skim milk, soy milk, plain or flavored low-fat yogurt, frozen low-fat yogurt, or soft silken tofu.

· In addition to the classic juices, such as OJ and apple juice, try tangerine juice, peach nectar, cranberry juice mix, or some of the new fruit blends.

· You can freeze smoothies in pop molds, ice cube trays, or paper cups. I also regularly pack smoothies in a thermos for school lunches.

sugar cookie dough

We've tried a lot of sugar cookie recipes over the years and found this one to be the best. It works especially well for these candy-filled cookies since, unlike store-bought dough, it holds its shape when baked.

YOU WILL NEED

❏ 1 cup unsalted butter, softened
❏ ¾ cup sugar
❏ 1 large egg
❏ 1 teaspoon vanilla extract
❏ ¼ teaspoon salt
❏ 2½ cups flour

1. Using an electric mixer at medium-high speed, cream the butter, gradually adding the sugar. Beat in the egg until evenly mixed, then blend in the vanilla extract and salt.

2. With a wooden spoon, stir the flour into the creamed ingredients, about one third at a time, until evenly blended. The dough may seem soft, but it will firm up when refrigerated.

3. Divide the dough in half. Flatten each portion into a disk and seal in plastic wrap. Refrigerate overnight.

windowpane hearts

MAKES: 30 | PREP TIME: 40 MINUTES | BAKE TIME: 8-10 MINUTES PER BATCH

A Valentine's Day celebration is one occasion when "cookie cutter" can actually mean "unique," thanks to these eye-catching candy-center cookies. And what drink goes well with these tasty treats? Why, pink milk, of course!

1. Heat the oven to 375°. Cover a sturdy baking sheet with aluminum foil and lightly coat the foil with cooking spray. Between 2 sheets of waxed paper lightly dusted with flour, roll the Sugar Cookie Dough (see recipe above) to a ¼-inch thickness. Remove the top sheet.

2. Cut out the cookies with a large cookie cutter. Use a spatula to transfer the shapes to the baking sheet, leaving about an inch between cookies. Remove the centers of the cookies with a smaller cookie cutter. (Save the centers to bake later.)

3. Place a hard candy (we used Jolly Ranchers) in the center of each heart and bake until the cookies start to brown lightly around the edges and the candy is melted, about 8 to 10 minutes. Let the cookies cool on the baking sheet for 5 minutes, then transfer them to wire racks to cool completely. To prevent sticking, line your serving plate or tin with waxed paper and place additional waxed paper between layers.

hugs-and-kisses cookies

MAKES: 10-30 | **PREP TIME:** 40 MINUTES | **CHILL TIME:** 2-3 HOURS | **BAKE TIME:** 8-12 MINUTES PER BATCH

This year, butter up your sweethearts with a batch of sugar-cookie hugs and kisses. Make bite-size X's and O's for a bunch of friends or a pair or giant letters for a special sweetie.

YOU WILL NEED

❑ Sugar Cookie Dough (see recipe at left)

Buttercream Icing:

❑ ¼ cup sifted confectioners' sugar

❑ ½ cup butter, softened

❑ ½ teaspoon vanilla extract

❑ 1 to 2 tablespoons milk

Optional:

❑ Colored sugar

1. Prepare the cookie dough according to the directions.

2. Divide the dough into 2 equal portions and flatten each into a disk. Cover each disk in plastic wrap and refrigerate for 2 to 3 hours, or until the dough is firm enough to work with. If it becomes too firm, soften at room temperature for about 5 minutes.

3. Preheat the oven to 350°. On a floured surface, roll out the dough to a ¼-inch thickness. Then, use a butter knife to cut out the cookies into X's and O's. Remind your child that giant letters need to be wider than smaller ones to keep them from breaking easily.

4. Using a metal spatula, carefully transfer the cookies to a baking sheet, leaving about 2 inches between them. Bake for 8 to 10 minutes (longer for really big cookies) or until lightly browned around the edges.

5. Remove the cookie sheets from the oven, place on wire racks and cool for 2 to 3 minutes. Using a metal spatula, transfer the cookies to the rack and cool completely. Makes about 3 dozen cookies, depending on their size.

6. While the cookies are cooling, make the buttercream icing: Beat together the sugar, butter, and vanilla extract. Add the milk a few drops at a time until the mixture is spreadable. Makes 1½ cups.

7. Frost the cookies with the icing and sprinkle on tinted red or pink sugar, if desired.

watermelon hearts

Move over, Cupid. These edible valentines will win the heart of everyone in the family. They're also sure to be a hit as a classroom snack. Use a heart-shaped cookie cutter on watermelon slices. Poke a bamboo kitchen skewer through each heart, then complete the arrow with an orange slice tip and tail.

crispy sweets

MAKES: 7 | **PREP TIME:** 30 MINUTES

Whip up a batch of tasty, crispy Valentine's Day goodies! This colorful new twist on a classic treat is a great gift for your child to give to anyone she's sweet on this February 14th.

YOU WILL NEED

❏ Cooking spray
❏ 3 tablespoons margarine
❏ 6 cups mini (or 60 regular-size) marshmallows
❏ Red food coloring
❏ 9 cups Rice Krispies cereal
❏ Heart-shaped cookie cutter
❏ Plastic bags, yarn

1. To begin, lightly coat a 10- by 15-inch baking sheet with cooking spray and set it aside.

2. Melt the margarine in a large pot over low heat. Add the marshmallows, stirring them continuously until they melt. Remove the pan from the heat.

3. Stir in drops of red food coloring until the color receives a thumbs-up from the chef. Add the Rice Krispies, stirring until they are evenly coated with marshmallow. Spoon the mixture onto the baking sheet. With waxed paper (or lightly buttered hands), smooth out the mixture, spreading it to an even thickness.

4. Now cut out hearts with the cookie cutter. Place each heart in a clear plastic bag, tie on a yarn bow, and it's ready for giving.

puppy love

Show your affection with a silly snack of hot-dog hearts. For each one, cut the ends from a cooked hot dog at a diagonal and place the cut edges together as shown. Spear the heart with a length of uncooked linguini. Add pieces of cheese trimmed to resemble the ends of an arrow.

whoopie pies

MAKES: 18 PIES | **PREP TIME:** 30 MINUTES | **BAKE TIME:** 10 MINUTES PER BATCH

No one is certain who invented the whoopie pie; folks in both Pennsylvania Amish country and Maine have claimed it. As for the name, one theory is that it comes from children saying "whoopie!" upon finding the moist, chocolaty sweets in their lunch pails. Your kids can experience the same glee after baking their own—and with pink-tinted filling, the pies will elicit cries of joy on Valentine's Day.

YOU WILL NEED

For the cakes:

- ❏ 2 cups flour
- ❏ ½ cup unsweetened cocoa powder
- ❏ 1 teaspoon baking soda
- ❏ ½ teaspoon salt
- ❏ 1 cup buttermilk
- ❏ 1 teaspoon vanilla extract
- ❏ ½ cup softened butter
- ❏ 1 cup sugar
- ❏ 1 egg

For the filling:

- ❏ ½ cup softened butter
- ❏ 1½ cups confectioners' sugar
- ❏ 1 cup marshmallow creme
- ❏ 1 teaspoon vanilla extract
- ❏ Red food coloring (optional)

1. Heat the oven to 350°. Line two baking sheets with parchment paper.

2. In a medium bowl, whisk together the flour, cocoa powder, baking soda, and salt. In a glass measuring cup or small bowl, stir together the buttermilk and vanilla extract.

3. In a large bowl with a hand mixer set at medium speed, beat the butter and sugar until evenly blended, about 1 to 2 minutes. Add the egg, increase the speed to high, and beat until smooth and creamy, about 1 minute more.

4. Pour half the flour mixture into the butter-sugar mixture, and beat at medium speed until combined. Add the buttermilk mixture and continue beating until just blended. Add the remaining flour mixture and beat again.

5. Use a cookie scoop (see below) or spoon to place a heaping tablespoon of batter on a prepared cookie sheet. Add more mounds of batter, evenly spacing them, until there are nine on each sheet. Slightly flatten each mound with a spoon.

6. Bake the cakes one sheet at a time for 10 minutes (they should be moist and spongy). Let them cool on the sheet for 2 minutes, then carefully transfer them to a rack to cool completely. Reline the sheets and scoop, shape, and bake the remaining batter.

7. Using an electric mixer at medium-high speed, beat all the filling ingredients except the coloring in a medium bowl until evenly blended, about 2 minutes. If you want to give the filling a Valentine hue, fold in drops of red food coloring until the desired tint is reached.

8. To make each pie, spoon and spread a heaping tablespoon of the filling onto the bottom of a cake, then gently press another cake on top.

valentine finger puppets

Young hearts (and fingers!) will dance at the sight of these lively paper puppets—which are a snap to make.

1. Cut a heart from colored card stock or heavy construction paper (use it as a template to make more).

2. Punch a starter hole for each finger with a hole punch, then use scissors to enlarge the circle; a child's fingers should fit snugly through the holes.

3. Decorate the heart with a paint pen or marker, adding facial features, and write your message on the back. Glue on googly eyes.

Message Ideas: I'm your puppet • You make my heart dance • Let's dance!

first-place treat

Everyone's a winner with these super-easy gold medals. To make one, sandwich two lengths of ribbon between gold stickers (we used Avery Notarial Labels). Cut an angled notch in each ribbon's tail. Write a message on the medal's front with permanent marker and use a glue dot to affix a foil-wrapped chocolate to the back.

Message Ideas: You take the prize • To a first-place friend • You've won my heart

sweetheart roses

Craft a bouquet of candy flowers for your buds.

The combination of candy and flowers is a surefire way to let someone know you're sweet on him or her. These valentines—pretty pink roses made from chocolate kisses—will cover you on both scores. With a little help, your kids can make enough to give to all their friends.

For each one, first form the bud by taping two foil-wrapped candies bottom to bottom. Drape a 5-inch square of pink plastic wrap over the top of one kiss, then gather the edges and twist them into a tail, as shown. Tightly twist the top of a green pipe cleaner around the tail for the stem.

At that point, add leaves by holding a strip of green tissue paper against the stem and rolling the pipe cleaner around the center of the strip. Trim the leaves so that they have pointy tips, and wrap green tape around the stem portion above the leaves to reinforce it.

monster mailbox

The only care these wild mailboxes require is a steady diet of Valentine's Day cards. This Alien Monster card holder is made from a **solid-color tissue box**. To bring this card-gobbler to life, **glue** soft **felt** teeth inside the box's opening and a **card stock** heart nose just above. Curl two **pipe cleaners** into springs by wrapping them around a **pen**, then glue a **1½-inch-wide googly eye** to the end of each spring. Insert the other ends through small holes in the box and secure them with **tape** inside.

valentine pencil toppers

Just like their edible cousins, these foam conversation hearts will let your child get right to the point of her Valentine's Day messages.

YOU WILL NEED

- ❏ Scissors
- ❏ Craft foam
- ❏ Permanent markers
- ❏ Pipe cleaner
- ❏ Pencil

1. Cut a 1- to 2-inch heart from craft foam.

2. With a permanent marker, print a short message on the front and the name of the giver on back.

3. Now poke an inch of the pipe cleaner through the bottom of the heart, bend it down, and twist it back around the remaining length of pipe cleaner. Coil the pipe cleaner tightly around the pencil. Then gently pull up on the heart so that part of the coil bobs freely above the pencil with several loops anchored around the eraser end.

heart flakes

Create a flurry of Valentine's Day decorations with this easy, heart-filled paper-snowflake technique.

Simply fold a piece of **origami paper** (we used the standard 5⅞-inch squares) in half diagonally, then in half twice more, as shown. Fold the resulting triangle so that the short folded edge meets the long folded edge. Draw a curve and a notch as shown, and carefully **cut** them out. Unfold. Cut carefully to avoid snipping off the point.

animal cards

With a handful of paper hearts, your child can round up some of these unforgettable elephants or romantic rodents to relay his Valentine's Day messages.

YOU WILL NEED

❏ Scissors

❏ Thin cardboard

❏ Pencil

❏ Colored paper or card stock

❏ Glue stick

❏ Googly eyes and stickers

❏ Pushpin

❏ Ribbon or string

❏ Colored markers

1. Cut a heart-shaped template, about 2½ inches high by 2½ inches wide, out of thin cardboard. Your child can trace around it in pencil to make the pieces he'll need.

2. To make a mouse, cut out 2 colored paper or card stock hearts (one for the body, one for the head) and glue them together, as shown. To accent the ears, glue a different shade of paper semicircles to the upper curves of the head. Then fold the ears so they'll stand upright. Attach googly eyes and a sticker nose. Use the pushpin to make a hole for the tail. Thread ribbon or string through it and knot the ends to keep them from slipping back through. Lastly, print a Valentine's Day message on the mouse's body.

3. For an elephant, trace around the template, then, before cutting out the shape, draw a curved trunk that extends directly from the bottom of the heart. Cut out the head as one piece and flip it over so the pencil lines won't show. Glue the tips of 2 heart-shaped ears to the back of the head. Attach googly eyes and decorative stickers. Then add your message.

gnome sweet gnome

These cuties are a cinch to mass-produce, and each gnome sweetens the deal with a chocolate kiss under its colorful hat. Plus, as one reader told us, "Anything with glitter or googly eyes is always a hit."

YOU WILL NEED (FOR 1)

❏ 3-inch-diameter can

❏ 4-inch square of felt

❏ Scissors

❏ Nontoxic glue such as Kid's Choice

❏ Paper clip

❏ Hershey's Kiss

❏ 2 (7-mm) googly eyes, adhesive-backed or not

❏ Pen or marker

❏ ¾-inch office dot sticker

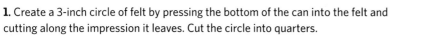

1. Create a 3-inch circle of felt by pressing the bottom of the can into the felt and cutting along the impression it leaves. Cut the circle into quarters.

2. To form the hat, run a thin line of glue along a straight edge of one felt quarter and press it to the other straight edge. Use a paper clip to hold the edges in place. When the glue is dry, remove the clip. Save the other quarters to make hats for more gnomes.

3. Glue the hat in place on the Hershey's Kiss, then stick or glue on the eyes. (Tip: You won't need much glue. We used a toothpick to apply the eye glue.) Allow the glue to dry. Use a pen or marker to write on a dot sticker and press it to the bottom of the Hershey's Kiss.

heartstring decoration

Transform cardboard tubes into love tokens to display as a mantel garland or door decoration.

YOU WILL NEED

- ❑ Cardboard tube (paper towel)
- ❑ Paintbrush and red paint
- ❑ Pushpin
- ❑ Needle
- ❑ Embroidery thread
- ❑ Beads (with holes large enough for the needle to pass through)

1. Cut the tube in thirds and brush the pieces inside and out with red paint. Let them dry.

2. Flatten the tubes, then cut them into one-inch segments. Shape each segment into a heart by pushing one creased side toward the center. Pierce holes in the top and bottom of each heart with a pushpin.

3. Thread the needle and knot the end. Slide on a bead until it stops at the knotted end, then loop back and push the needle through the bead again, going from bottom to top. Thread on a heart, then add a bead just above it, using the same looping technique to secure it in place. Repeat to create a string of hearts and beads.

puppy card

Assemble a litter of these puppies, and your child's friends will howl with pleasure. With a candy tongue, they're doggone cute and clever!

1. Cut a large heart from card stock (ours is about 4½ inches wide). Cut 2 smaller, elongated heart-shaped ears from a different shade of card stock, and a small heart nose from red card stock.

2. Glue the ears, nose, and googly eyes to the large heart.

3. Tape a piece of candy (we used a small Kit Kat) to the back so that one end sticks out below the mouth like a tongue. (We rounded the edges of ours with scissors.) If you like, add a message to the back or the ears with markers.

card carrier

Once all the notes have been signed, sealed, and delivered, your child can use this pretty paper satchel to tote home all the messages she's received.

1. Start with 2 sheets of decorative 8½-by-11-inch scrapbook paper. Cut a 1-inch-wide strip from a short end of one of the sheets and set it aside. Then tape or glue together the 2 sheets at their short ends, overlapping the papers by about ½ inch. Once the glue has dried, fold the papers as shown, creating an 8-inch flap and a 4-inch flap, then trim the smaller flap to a point.

2. To make a closure, unfold and use a craft knife to cut 2 horizontal 1¼-inch slits in the front panel as shown, then glue a small craft foam or construction paper heart between the slits. Cut the 1-inch-wide strip in two, then glue one half to the underside of the top flap and trim it to a point.

3. Finally, seal the sides of the larger flap with glue to create a pouch and let all the glue dry completely.

friendship rings

These flashy rings let a kid wear her heart on her finger.
Tip: If you make your ring from craft foam, you won't need a
hole punch; simply poke the pipe cleaner through the foam.

YOU WILL NEED
- ❏ Scissors
- ❏ Craft foam or card stock
- ❏ Faux fur fabric (optional)
- ❏ White glue
- ❏ Small hole punch
- ❏ Pipe cleaner
- ❏ Faux jewels, buttons, craft foam shapes, etc.
- ❏ Marker or pen (optional)

1. Cut a 1" to 1½" heart shape from craft foam or card stock. If you use fabric,
first glue a small piece of the fabric to foam or card stock, allow the glue to dry,
then cut out the heart shape.

2. Unless you're working with foam, use a small hole punch to make 2 holes, centered, in the heart.
Cut a 4-inch length of pipe cleaner. Bend it in half and push the ends through the holes from front
to back as shown.

3. Place the ring on your child's finger to measure the size. Twist the pipe cleaner ends together until
the ring fits comfortably. Remove the ring and trim and tuck any excess pipe cleaner.

4. Glue on faux jewels, buttons, craft foam shapes, or other items for decoration. Allow the glue to dry.
Use a marker or pen to write a few words on the back of the ring, if you like.

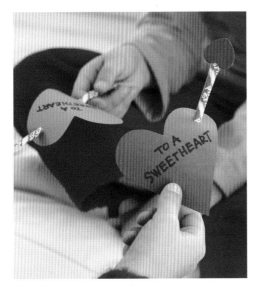

sweet hearts

We're fond of these valentines because they're simple, fun, and inexpensive.

YOU WILL NEED
- ❏ Scissors
- ❏ Card stock
- ❏ Hole punch
- ❏ Marker
- ❏ Pixy Stix
- ❏ Stickers

1. Cut a heart from card stock (ours are
3½-inches wide and 3½-inches tall). Punch 2
holes in the heart, one toward the upper right
and one toward the lower left. Use markers to
add a message.

2. Insert a Pixy Stix powdered candy straw
through one of the holes. Gently bend the card
and slide the straw out through the other hole.

3. To make the arrow, sandwich 2 heart-shaped
stickers (we got ours from Oriental Trading
Company) over each end of the Pixy Stix.

social butterfly

This clever candy messenger with beating heart-shaped wings is sure to bring even the shiest valentine out of his cocoon. Your kids will be amazed as a stack of candy sticks and colored paper quickly metamorphoses into a class-size bunch of unique cards.

YOU WILL NEED

- ❏ 4"x6" piece of card stock or cardboard
- ❏ Pencil
- ❏ Scissors
- ❏ 4"x6" piece of construction paper or colored card stock
- ❏ 1 old-fashioned candy stick, in a wrapper
- ❏ 1 10-inch pipe cleaner
- ❏ 4 color-coding sticker dots (available at office supply stores)
- ❏ Marker

1. Begin by making a template for the wings: fold the cardboard rectangle in half and, from the folded seam, cut out the top two thirds of a heart (think *butterfly*—it may help to draw the shape before you begin cutting). Open up the template, then have your kids trace around it onto the construction paper or colored card stock and cut out the wings.

2. Now create slots for the candy-stick body: fold the wings back in half and make two ½-inch cuts, ½ inch apart, across the middle of the folded seam. Open the wings and weave the candy stick down into one slit and up through the other.

3. To make the antennae, wind the pipe cleaner tightly around one end of the candy stick so that two equal lengths extend upward, and then curl the ends. Finally, decorate your butterfly with the sticker dots and write your message on the back.

Assembly line tips: One child can trace the wings while another cuts them out. Then, after the bodies are assembled, one child can wrap the pipe cleaners and the other can curl their ends.

spin art heart

Nothing makes the head spin like love—except, perhaps, this valentine, which is an update on the county fair favorite, spin art. Simply place a paper plate flat in a salad spinner, dribble in any water-based paint, and start cranking the handle. Remove from the spinner, let dry overnight, and cut into a heart shape (use specialty scissors to make a fancy border). Inscribe the back to your valentine.

friendship blossoms

Here, two classic Valentine's Day gifts—flowers and candy—combine to make one sweet treat. For each, cut three heart-shaped petals, two leaves, and two floral-shaped flower centers from **scrapbooking paper** or **card stock.** Poke a small hole in each, crease the petals as shown, and slide the pieces onto the stem of a **lollipop. Tape** the bottom to secure.

To: Sue
From: Lucy

guppy love

Fishing for compliments this Valentine's Day? These little swimmers made of hearts should earn oceans of praise.

1. From colored card stock or heavy construction paper, cut 2 large heart shapes for the fish's body and 1 small heart for the tail.

2. Glue together the 3 hearts to make a fish shape, as shown.

3. Use a paint pen or marker to write a message on the back, then add a mouth and a googly eye to the front.

Message Ideas: Best fishes this Valentine's Day! You're my fish in the sea • You're oceans of fun! May your fishes come true this Valentine's Day

scratch and win valentines

Everyone can hit the jackpot with these lottery-inspired valentines featuring messages hidden beneath scratch-off hearts.

1. To make 36 hearts, combine 2 tablespoons of metallic acrylic paint and 1 tablespoon of dishwashing liquid in a disposable container. With a foam brush, paint a thin coating of the mixture onto the nonadhesive side of a 13-inch square of clear contact paper. When the coating is dry, add two more coats, letting each dry thoroughly.

2. Next, download our templates from FamilyFun.com/magazine. Print the Lucky Lotto page onto card stock and cut out the tickets. Using our heart template as a guide, cut hearts from the painted contact paper.

3. Write a message on the right-hand side of each ticket. Peel the backing from a painted heart and stick it in place over the note. If you like, glue each ticket to a 3-by-6-inch rectangle of card stock and decorate it with 3-D paint pens.

jolly lollies

Our silly suckers are part treat, part toy. And whether your child chooses the hilarious mustachioed pop or the lolly-puckered mouth, he'll have found a witty way to say: "Read my lips: I like you!"

YOU WILL NEED

- ❏ Red or brown permanent marker
- ❏ Red, pink, or brown craft foam
- ❏ Scissors
- ❏ Craft knife or small hole punch to match the size of your lollipop stick (we used a ⅛-inch punch; punches available at many craft stores)
- ❏ Wrapped lollipop
- ❏ Pen
- ❏ White office label

1. Use a marker to draw a mustache or lips onto craft foam. Cut out the shape with scissors.

2. To slide the lollipop through the foam, make a hole using a small punch as shown or make a tiny slit with a craft knife (a parent's job). Slip the lollipop through the hole. Next, cut the label in half if necessary, write a message on it, and fold it around the stick.

To Dawn From Pete

sweet text message

Cupid's calling! And we've got the perfect answer: a candy-button phone that tells your valentines they're worth every minute. To make one, simply cut a rectangle from **silver card stock** (ours is about 2½ by 7 inches), then fold it in half and round the corners. **Glue** on two **paper** message screens and a **sheet of button candy** for a keypad.

forget-me-not elephant

Trust this clever little pachyderm to deliver an unforgettable message. Not only does each elephant have a great memory for love poems (he keeps your child's sweet nothings stashed away safely in his ears, which slide out and unfold into heart shapes), but he's also hiding a candy present to sweeten the deal.

YOU WILL NEED

❑ Pencil
❑ Colored art paper or construction paper
❑ Scissors
❑ Craft knife
❑ 1 sheet of white paper
❑ Marker
❑ Glue stick
❑ Tape (optional)
❑ Small piece of wrapped candy (optional)

1. Draw an elephant silhouette onto a folded sheet of art paper or print one out from our website (www.familyfun.com).

2. Cut out the elephant (being careful not to cut through the fold at the top of its back) and then use a craft knife to cut two small slits on each side of the head (a parent's job).

3. Cut two little paper hearts from white paper and write a message on one side. Fold the hearts in half lengthwise and slip them through the slits to form the elephant's ears and tusks.

4. Glue the trunks together at the tip.

5. For an added surprise, tape a wrapped candy inside the elephant.

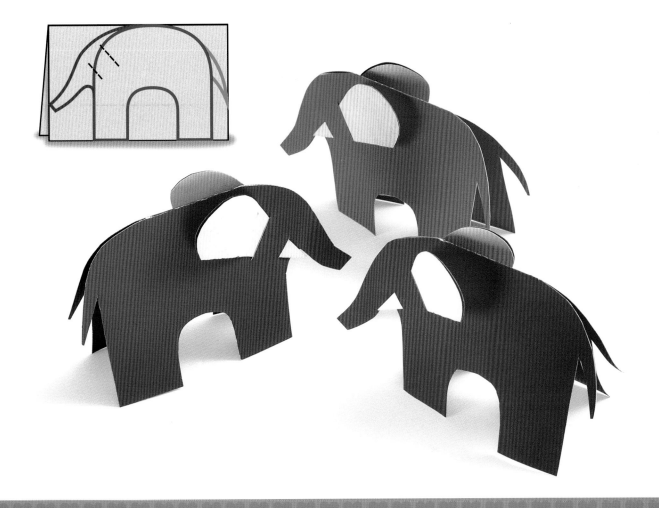

sweet shovel valentine

What's the scoop? Just a sweets-laden toy shovel that's perfect for a kid's sandbox pals.

1. Close a small bag of candy with a twist tie. With a ribbon, tie it to the handle of a toy sand shovel. (We found a good selection of shovels at www.iparty.com for 40 cents apiece.)

2. Use a paint pen or permanent marker to write your message at the base of the shovel, just below the candy bag.

Message Ideas: I dig you! • Here's the scoop on Valentine's Day • It's Valentine's Day—dig it! • You've got the scoop on me!